CEREMONIAL COSTUMES

Other books in this series include:

Military Uniforms
Carol Harris and Mike Brown

Accessories
Carol Harris and Mike Brown

Children's Costumes
Carol Harris and Mike Brown

Women's Costumes
Carol Harris and Mike Brown

Men's Costumes
Carol Harris and Mike Brown

Festivals
Ellen Galford

North American Dress
Dr. Louise Aikman

The Performing Arts
Alycen Mitchell

Everyday Dress
Chris McNab

Rescue Services
Carol Harris and Mike Brown

Religious Costumes
Ellen Galford

TWENTIETH-CENTURY DEVELOPMENTS IN FASHION AND COSTUME

CEREMONIAL COSTUMES

LEWIS LYONS

MASON CREST PUBLISHERS

www.masoncrest.com

Mason Crest Publishers Inc.
370 Reed Road
Broomall, PA 19008
(866) MCP-BOOK (toll free)
www.masoncrest.com

First printing 2002

1 2 3 4 5 6 7 8 9 10

Library of Congress Cataloging-in-Publication Data available

ISBN 1-59084-424-6

Printed and bound in Malaysia

Editorial and design by
Amber Books Ltd.
Bradley's Close
74–77 White Lion Street
London N1 9PF

Project Editor: Marie-Claire Muir
Designer: Zoe Mellors
Picture Research: Lisa Wren

Picture Credits:
Amber Books Ltd: 5 (top right), 41 **Corbis:** 54, 56 **The Culture Archive:** 12, 24, 26, 53 **Popperfoto:** 5 (left and bottom right), 8, 9, 10, 15, 17, 27, 31, 32, 33, 35, 39, 42, 44, 45, 47, 48. **Topham:** 6, 18, 20, 22, 28, 50
Cover images: The Culture Archive: main, background, and bottom left; **Popperfoto:** top left

Acknowledgment:
For authenticating this book, the Publishers would like to thank
JONES NEW YORK.

Contents

Introduction

Every day we go to our closets with the same question in mind: what shall I wear today? Clothing can convey status, wealth, occupation, religion, sexual orientation, and social, political, and moral values. The clothes we wear affect how we are perceived and also reflect what image we want to project.

Fashion has always been influenced by the events, people, and places that shape society. The 20th century was a period of radical change, encompassing two world wars, suffrage, a worldwide Depression, the invention of "talkies" and the rise of Hollywood, the birth of the teenager, the global spread of television, and, later, the World Wide Web, to name just a few important developments. Politically, economically, technologically, and socially, the world was changing at a fast and furious pace. Fashion, directly influenced by all these factors, changed with them, leaving each period with its fashion icon.

The 1920s saw the flapper reign supreme, with her short dress and cropped, boyish hair. The '30s and '40s brought a wartime mindset: women entered the workforce en masse and traded their silk stockings for nylon. During the conservative 1950s—typified by twin sets and capri pants—a young Elvis Presley took the world by storm. The '60s gave us PVC, miniskirts, and mods, and in 1967, the Summer of Love spawned a new language of fashion in which bell-bottoms and tie-dyed shirts became political expressions of peace and love. In the 1980s, power and affluence became the hallmarks of a new social group, the yuppies. Designer branding led the way, and the slogan "Nothing comes between me and my Calvins" started an era of status dressing. The 1990s will be best remembered for a new fashion word introduced by the underground street and music movement of Seattle, grunge.

Twentieth-Century Developments in Fashion and Culture is a 12-volume, illustrated series that looks at changing fashions throughout this eventful century, and encourages readers to question what the clothes they wear reveal about themselves and the world they live in.

Special introduction and consultation:
JONES NEW YORK

Souvenir of the CORONATION 12th May 1937.

CANADA
S.AFRICA
INDIA
CEYLON
AUSTRALIA
NEW ZEALAND

LONG LIVE the KING!

CHAPTER 1

Royalty

The 20th century was an age of democracy, with less room for kings and queens. Modern monarchs have had to adapt to changing circumstances, and this change is reflected in royal clothing.

As of this writing—at the beginning of the 21st century—there are monarchs in Africa, Asia, Europe, the Middle East, and Oceania, but few have any real power. Although royal robes are worn at coronations, monarchs often attend official functions wearing the same business suits as any politician.

In her book *The Language of Clothes*, Alison Lurie lists the ways in which clothing is used to indicate wealth and status. These are all displayed in royal clothing.

King George VI of Britain (left) is shown in 1937, the year of his coronation. He was the last king to hold the title "Emperor of India." British Foreign Secretary Anthony Eden (right) is in full court dress, on the way to a reception with the king.

- **Layered clothing.** Ceremonial robes used at coronations are multilayered, in contrast to the simpler clothing worn by the average person.
- **Expensive, rare, and fine materials, such as handwoven silks and precious furs.** The rarity of the animal pelt indicates the high status of the wearer. Whereas a peasant might wear leather and a hunter wear fox, a king or queen wears **ermine** or lion.
- **The wearing of wealth itself, in the form of jewels and precious metals.** This includes such items as crowns, orbs, and **scepters**, and clothes sewn with gold.
- **Excess materials, in the form of flowing robes and long trains.** Princess Diana's wedding dress was of conventional design except in one respect—its extravagant 25-foot- (7.6-m-) long train.

Royal clothing displays much more than wealth. Royal clothing is special; it denotes the rank of the wearer and can only be worn by the monarch. In England, there were once "sumptuary laws" that forbade people to wear noble or royal clothing—that is, expensive or ostentatious—if they were not of the appropriate social rank.

Royal clothing is loaded with symbolism. Coronation garments often contain elements that symbolize the monarch's powers and the extent of his or her territories. Elizabeth II's coronation dress, for example, was embroidered with floral

Queen Alexandra of Britain became queen in 1901. An elegant dresser, and still slender at the age of 58, she had been influencing fashions since she introduced the "princess dress" in 1863.

emblems of all the **Commonwealth** nations. Other decorative elements may indicate the rank of the wearer. In the coronation robes worn by the British nobility, the number and position of the black spots on the white fur capes indicate the seniority of the wearer.

Coronation ceremonies around the world are surprisingly similar. The literal meaning of *coronation* is "crowning," and the placing of a crown on the monarch's head is the final act of a ceremony that consists of investing (literally, "dressing") the monarch in clothing that symbolizes the powers being granted to him or her.

QUEEN ALEXANDRA

On the death of Queen Victoria in 1901, Princess Alexandra became queen when her husband was crowned Edward VII of Britain. She had always been an elegant and fashionable dresser, first wearing the "princess dress," fitted at the waist with a row of buttons down the front, in 1863.

By 1902, the **belle-epoque** style had arrived, with a taste for sumptuous display and loose, flimsy fabrics. Though she was 58 when she became queen, Alexandra had kept her youthful figure and was well suited to the style.

In 1907, she wore an embroidered gold **tulle** state gown for the state visit of the German king. The dress was in one piece, including train and scarf sleeves, of pale yellow tulle **appliqué** embroidered with gold-**tissue** flowers, tissue bands under the tulle, and gold sequins and flowers, with pale yellow satin and **chiffon** foundations.

Like her granddaughter-in-law Princess Diana, Alexandra followed and influenced the high fashion of her day. Alexandra's wardrobe was sold at auction in 1937 in New York City. The prices fetched by Alexandra's wardrobe were no match for Diana's when her wardrobe was auctioned off for millions of dollars. Alexandra's gold tulle state gown was in the sale catalog at a **reserve** of $45—equivalent to only $570 today.

THE CORONATION OF QUEEN ELIZABETH II

The robes that Queen Elizabeth II wore at her coronation in 1953 were a mixture of innovation and tradition stretching back to the 13th century.

British designer Norman Hartnell designed the queen's coronation dress. It was of white satin, covered in thousands of tiny seed pearls and crystals, each in a silver setting, arranged in a latticework effect. It was sleeveless, and had a fitted bodice and a full, flaring skirt. The neckline was cut in a heart shape in the center. The robe was lined with pure silk English satin and trimmed with a five-inch-(13-cm-) wide band of Canadian ermine. It had a train of six yards (5.5 m) of purple velvet and an embroidered ermine cape.

Three embroidered and jeweled bands running across the skirt depicted floral emblems of the United Kingdom and the Commonwealth. There were Tudor roses for England; thistles for Scotland; shamrocks for Northern Ireland; leeks for Wales; two different lotuses for India and Sri Lanka; protea for South Africa; wattle (acacia) flower for Australia; wheat, cotton, and jute for Pakistan; maple leaves for Canada; and fern for New Zealand.

Queen Elizabeth II is in her coronation dress by British designer Norman Hartnell. It is embroidered with plants and flowers representing each of the Commonwealth nations.

The coronation dress and floral symbols were entirely new, and all the clothing used in the coronation was made especially for the ceremony. But the design of some of the garments was centuries old, and all played a specific symbolic role. For example, the first item placed on the monarch in a British coronation is the *colobium sindonis*, a loose, sleeveless gown of white cambric that has been used since at least the coronation of Edward the Confessor in 1272. It is similar to the simple gowns worn by all classes at the time, and symbolizes the fact that the monarch's authority derives from the people.

When Princess Elizabeth entered Westminster Abbey as heir to the throne, she wore the crimson "Parliament gown." At the end of the ceremony, her Parliament gown was removed, and the purple robe of state was placed on the newly crowned Queen Elizabeth II. Only a reigning monarch wears the purple robe of state. It is emblematic of the imperial purple worn by the Caesars of ancient Rome and later adopted by the Byzantine and Holy Roman emperors.

The purple robe of state has not been used since the coronation. The queen prefers to use the less-formal Parliament gown at such occasions as the State Opening of Parliament, which marks the start of each year's parliamentary session.

PRINCESS DIANA

When the reserved 19-year-old Lady Diana Spencer first met the press, she was awkward with the reporters and committed a grave error by posing for photographers in a lightweight skirt that turned see-through against the sunlight. During her marriage to Prince Charles and after her separation and divorce, Diana worked hard to ensure she never made such a mistake in her dress or in her handling of the press again.

When Diana married Charles in 1981, Britain was in a recession, and the royal family was seen as out of touch and irrelevant. As an outsider, Diana was able to shake up the royal family, modernizing their image and bringing them some much-needed glamour.

Perhaps the most famous of all Diana's dresses is her long-trained white wedding dress by British designers David and Elizabeth Emmanuel. The dress was modern, but the excess of its 25-foot- (7.6-m-) long train, held by uniformed pages as she walked, unmistakably symbolized the high status of the wearer.

Diana made a point of frequenting British designers, such as Zandra Rhodes, Bruce Oldfield, Catherine Walker, and the Emmanuels. The Emmanuels also designed the famous black dress with plunging neckline that she wore for her first public engagement with Prince Charles.

Diana knew how to make a statement with her clothing. On the night that British television aired an interview with Prince Charles giving his side of the story of their failed marriage, Diana attended a party and posed for photographers in a daringly short black cocktail dress by British designer Christina Stambolian. Pictures of her in what the press dubbed the "Up-Yours" dress appeared in all the following day's papers.

After her divorce, Diana posed for a celebrated photo shoot by Mario Testino for *Vanity Fair* magazine, wearing a low-cut dress and casual clothes, and looking relaxed and happy to be away from the stuffy confines of the royal family. At the same time, she literally threw off her royal vestments by auctioning off her vast collection of formal dresses.

BRITISH COURT DRESS

In the British royal court, people attending court occasions or meeting royalty wore special clothing. Upper-class girls and boys were "presented at court" to mark their entry into adult social life. Girls were presented at a ceremony called a Drawing Room, which took place at Buckingham Palace, and boys were presented at a Levée, at nearby St. James' Palace.

At the turn of the 20th century, gentlemen wore military-style court uniforms, introduced by George IV in 1820. These were made of fine wool and decorated with embroidery and gold and silver wire.

GOING, GOING, GONE

On June 25, 1997, a collection of 79 of Diana's dresses was auctioned at Christie's in New York City to benefit a range of charities, including the AIDS Crisis Trust and the Royal Marsden Hospital Cancer Fund. The magnetic appeal of royal clothing, even in the modern age, seems to be undiminished—the auction raised $3.2 million. The majority of the buyers—an impressive 83 percent—were from the United States.

The most expensive dress went for $225,000, the highest price ever paid for a garment sold at auction. Diana wore the blue dress for a 1985 White House state dinner with President Ronald Reagan and was photographed in it dancing with John Travolta. Interestingly, the previous top auction price for a garment was for the white suit that John Travolta wore in *Saturday Night Fever*.

Diana's dresses have continued to exert power over people even after her death. In 1998, 20 of Diana's gowns were displayed in a two-year international tour, which raised tens of millions of dollars for charity, strong evidence of the power of the modern cult of celebrity.

Ladies wore modified versions of 18th-century court dress, which included heavily embroidered silk **bodices** and trains, ostrich-feather headdresses, and lace veils. Many of these elements remained in fashion until as late as 1939. The color of the cloth and the style of the embroidery were used to distinguish the rank and position of the wearer.

The details of court uniforms were so numerous and complex that, from the end of the 19th century, the Lord Chamberlain issued a periodically updated set of regulations explaining the proper dress to be worn by officials of every rank and office. The last of these, "Dress and Insignia Worn at His Majesty's Court," was published in 1936.

The **Victorian** and **Edwardian** passion for uniforms extended beyond the royal court into government and civil society. There were five—and after World War I, six—classes of civil uniforms, covering such positions as Master of the Horse and Pages of Honor. There were also military uniforms, which were worn by governors and high commissioners, as well as military officers.

After World War II, attendees at court were no longer required to wear court dress. With the relaxing of dress regulations, British designers, such as Norman Hartnell, made their reputations by designing spectacular dresses to be worn at royal occasions. Hartnell's distinctive embroidered and beaded dresses were a success at Buckingham Palace and brought him numerous new customers, including Queen Elizabeth herself.

EMPEROR HIROHITO

Hirohito (1901–1989), the 124th emperor of Japan, succeeded to the throne in 1926 and saw his country through humiliating defeat in World War II and on to a postwar economic boom. Like all Japanese emperors before him, Hirohito had the status of a god when he came to the throne. On January 1, 1946, five months after the end of the war, Hirohito announced to his people that the emperor was no longer to be considered divine. Under the new Japanese

TROOPING THE COLOR

This ceremony dates from the 18th century, when colors were carried through the ranks so that soldiers could later recognize them in battle, but the lavish public parade that takes place in England every year is a 20th-century invention. The ceremony was private until Edward VII (1901–1910) started the tradition of riding at the head of the Guards (the regiment or batallion assigned to protect the monarch) in full dress uniform, a tradition that has continued in England to this day.

The popular spectacle has been copied by other monarchs around the world. King Bhumibol Adulyadej of Thailand, for example, also has a Trooping the Color ceremony to mark his birthday (pictured below). The royal guard regiment's colors are trooped before the king and there is a colorful military parade through the streets of Bangkok.

Trooping the Color has become so popular that some republics have even adopted it. In Romania, for example, there is an annual Trooping the Color parade, where the regimental banner is paraded before the president and a group of invited dignitaries.

constitution that was part of Japan's postwar settlement, the emperor became a head of state without any real powers.

On his accession to the throne, Hirohito wore the 19th-century ceremonial military uniform that his father, Emperor Meiji, had introduced to replace the 10th-century ritual robes worn by his predecessors. Just one month after Japan's

Emperor Hirohito of Japan waves to the crowd during his 1946 tour of his country. He has abandoned his traditional robes in favor of a Western-style suit.

surrender, Hirohito entered the American embassy dressed in a **morning suit** to discuss Japan's postwar settlement with General Douglas MacArthur. In 1946, the no-longer-divine Hirohito went on an unprecedented tour to meet his people. The democratic monarch was now dressed in a stylish suit like any politician, waving his crumpled **fedora** to the crowds and shaking hands instead of bowing.

KING HUSSEIN I OF JORDAN

King Hussein I (1935–1999) was born Hussein bin Talal in Amman, Jordan. When he was 10 years old, Jordan gained independence from Britain and Hussein's grandfather Abdullah became the modern state's first king. While on a visit to Jerusalem with his grandfather in 1951, Abdullah was assassinated on the steps of the Al-Aqsa Mosque. The gunman also fired at Hussein, but the bullet bounced off a gold medal worn over his heart.

Hussein's father Talal then became king, and Hussein was sent to school in England. Talal suffered from schizophrenia and was declared unfit to rule. On August 11, 1952, 16-year old Hussein was proclaimed king, but a **regency** ruled Jordan until Hussein reached the age of 18. Meanwhile, the young king finished his education at England's Sandhurst Military College, where it is said the drill sergeants addressed him as "Mr. King Hussein, Sir."

The teenage king took his job seriously. As he later said in his autobiography, *Uneasy Lies the Head*: "I had seen enough of Europe even at 17 to know that its playgrounds were filled with ex-kings, some of whom lost their thrones because they did not understand the duties of a monarch. I was not going to become a permanent member of their swimming parties in the south of France."

Although Hussein was from a royal line that dates back to the time of the Prophet Muhammad, Hussein wore a ceremonial military uniform rather than royal robes at his coronation. Throughout his reign, Hussein's style of dress reflected the modern conception of a democratic monarch. It also summed up

King Hussein of Jordan (right) wears a suit for peace talks with Yitzhak Rabin of Israel, in Washington, D.C., in 1994. A "modern" king who reached out to the West, King Hussein also championed Arab rights. In his dress, he often showed this by combining a suit with a traditional Jordanian headdress.

his dual policy of modernization and engagement with the West, while pursuing Jordanian and Arab influence in the Middle East.

When Hussein met Queen Elizabeth II during her state visit to Jordan in 1984, he wore a Western-style business suit with a *shmagh*, the traditional Jordanian headdress. Particularly in the later years of his reign, he wore a suit for meetings with political leaders, such as President Bush in 1989 and President Clinton in 1996.

EMPEROR HAILE SELASSIE I OF ETHIOPIA

Haile Selassie I (1892–1975), born Tafari Makonnen, was crowned emperor of Ethiopia in 1930. During the Italian occupation of Ethiopia (1936–1941) during World War I, he lived in exile in Britain. Haile was restored to the throne by the Allies at the end of the war and ruled until 1974, when he was deposed in a military **coup**.

He was a charismatic leader and statesman who made Ethiopia a prominent force in African affairs and helped establish the Organization of African Unity in the early 1960s. He is revered by the Rastafarian religion, which takes its name from him (Ras Tafari means "King Tafari").

In a lavish ceremony attended by representatives from 70 countries, Haile Selassie was crowned under a gold-encrusted, red velvet canopy in the open air, with four live lions chained to the corners of the dais. At the end of the ceremony, Haile donned a full-length robe of lion skins. He was anointed seven times by the archbishop of the ancient Coptic Church (the established religion of Ethiopia) and invested with seven symbols of his powers: gold-embroidered scarlet robes, a jeweled sword and ring, and a gold scepter, orb, and **lances**.

The Ethiopian royal family claims descent from the biblical King Solomon and the Queen of Sheba, and although elements of the coronation dated back to biblical times, the ceremony was, in fact, thoroughly modern. Tailors in London made the lion robe a few months before. According to a news report in *Time* magazine, a bale of lion skins was delivered with instructions "to fashion them into suitable garments for a coronation." The emperor was driven to the coronation in the coach that had belonged to Kaiser Wilhelm II, apparently snapped up in Germany for the bargain price of $6,000. Streets in Addis Ababa were paved, and electricity and telephone lines installed. The city police were dressed in khaki uniforms from Belgium, and a British naval band provided the music.

Emperor Haile Selassie I of Ethiopia is in a jeweled headdress of gold. Coronations had always been private affairs in Ethiopia, but Haile Selassie broke with tradition. His lavish public coronation was attended by representatives from over 70 countries.

The coronation marked a huge break with Ethiopian tradition. It had always been the custom for emperors to be crowned in private the day after the predecessor died. But Haile Selassie wanted Ethiopia to enter the world stage. As he says in his autobiography, *My Life and Ethiopia's Progress*:

"Now that Ethiopia had concluded treaties of commerce and friendship with twelve foreign governments, had entered the League of Nations, and had established firm friendly relations, We [sic] were convinced that it was proper—in accordance with the practice of the most civilized governments in the case of their coronations—to invite to Our [sic] coronation the countries which had set up legations and consulates in Ethiopia. But as it would require a long time to dispatch the letters of invitation and to await the arrival of the delegates, as well as to make all the necessary preparations for the coronation, We [sic] arranged for the ceremony to be postponed for seven months."

"EMPEROR" BOKASSA

Jean Bédel Bokassa (1921–1996) led a successful coup in the Central African Republic in 1966. Over the next few years, he steadily increased his personal power, becoming president-for-life in 1972, then, in 1977, self-styled emperor of his country, which he renamed the Central African Empire.

Bokassa's coronation was based on the coronation of Napoleon, and it is estimated to have cost over $25 million, a quarter of his country's annual income. Bokassa was surrounded by fine fabrics, gold, and jewels, and he sat on a gold-plated bronze throne in the form of an eagle, 11-feet (3.5-m) high and 8-feet (2.5-m) wide and weighing 2.2 tons (2 metric tons).

This extravagant waste did not endear him to the people of his poor country. He was already unpopular, and resistance to his rule increased after his coronation. Bokassa cracked down on his political opponents and is believed to have been responsible for many deaths. He was **deposed** and exiled in 1979, but returned unexpectedly in 1986, when he was tried and imprisoned for life.

KING BHUMIBOL ADULYADEJ OF THAILAND

King Bhumibol Adulyadej the Great came to the throne in 1946, following the death of his brother. The king displays a remarkable range of talents. He is a jazz musician and composer, has won gold medals for sailing, and is active in painting, photography, and engineering. He was given the title "the Great" by the Thai prime minister in 1988, after more than 40 million of Thailand's 55 million people voted to award him the honor.

"We will reign with righteousness, for the benefit and happiness of the Siamese people." Those words have been pronounced by each Thai king at his coronation, ever since the establishment of the first dynasty in the 13th century. The Thai concept of kingship has always included a duty to act for the benefit of the people—in contrast to other Asian and European monarchies who have believed in the absolute power of the ruler.

Self-styled "Emperor" Bokassa of the Central African Republic is shown here in a military uniform adorned with medals—however, it is less extravagent than the dress worn at his coronation.

At Bhumibol's coronation, May 5, 1950, at the Grand Palace, the king wore the Quintet of Royal Regalia, following a tradition that dates back to the Sukhothai Kingdom (13th–15th centuries), regarded by Thai historical tradition as the first Thai kingdom. The Royal Regalia reflects the Thai concept of kingship: not only investing the king with the outward brilliance of majesty and command, but it is also intended to remind the people of the king's burdens and his responsibilities to his subjects.

THE ROYAL REGALIA

The Royal Regalia, together with Royal Utensils and the Royal Eight Weapons of Sovereignty, are traditionally presented to the kings of Thailand at their coronation ceremonies.

The Royal Fan, or *Wan-wit-cha-ni*, is made from the talipot palm and is gilded and enameled in red and green. King Rama IV added a flywhisk made from the tail of a yak, but it became damaged over time and has been replaced by one made from the tail of an albino elephant, with a gilt and enamel handle.

The Royal Slippers, or *Cha long Phra Bat Choeng Ngon*, are made entirely of gold, tapering at the toes and with a red velvet lining.

The exquisite Great Crown of Victory, or *Phra Maha Phichai Mongkut*, is made in gold, enameled in red and green, and set with diamonds. The distinctly Thai design is conical, ending in a tapering spire, with large diamonds and flexible gold ornamentations that sway with the slightest movement. The crown is 26 inches (66 cm) tall and weighs 16 pounds (7.3 kg).

The jeweled Sword of Victory, or *Phra Saeng Khan Chai Si*, symbolizes the king's duty to protect his people. The Royal Staff, or *Than Phra Kon*, is made from cassia wood with gold ends and symbolizes the guiding of the king's footsteps on the path of justice.

CHAPTER 2

Political and Military Dress

Throughout the 20th century, political leaders have generally worn a suit, the standard global uniform of politics and business. Never ones to be fashion leaders, presidents strive to look modern but dignified, never too trendy.

John F. Kennedy's youthful good looks and fashionably tailored suits set him apart from a drab Richard Nixon in the televised debates and election campaign of 1960. In the 1970s, President Jimmy Carter was known, not so much for his wide-lapeled suits, as for

Mao Tse-Tung, Chairman of the Chinese Communist party, promoted the wearing of the blue "Mao" jacket by millions of Chinese people. Referred to as the "sea of blue," the Mao jacket was, in effect, a civilian uniform.

U.S. President Theodore Roosevelt was a vigorous man of action, who also knew the value of publicity and courting the press. Here, he was happy to pose in a hunting outfit for a photographer in 1902.

his work shirts, which emphasized his image as a Washington outsider from the peanut farms of Georgia.

Presidents and presidential hopefuls are aware of the importance of images that break with the usual convention of the business suit. These images are often carefully contrived to show the "real" man behind the suit. No election campaign is complete without an appearance in a hard hat at a construction site or in a sweatshirt volunteering at a soup kitchen.

THEODORE ROOSEVELT

In the early years of the 20th century, for the first time, events could be photographed as they happened and be printed in the next day's newspapers. Theodore Roosevelt—at that point the youngest American president there had ever been and a firm advocate of "the life of strenuous endeavor"—was the first president to grasp the importance of appealing directly to the people, not just by frequent public speaking, but also by cultivating a relationship with the press. Roosevelt was happy to pose for photographs in suitably vigorous attitudes. One press photograph from his 1904 campaign sums up the two images that Roosevelt was trying to get across: stable president and vigorous man of action. He is dressed in a "presidential" dark suit and tie, but mounted on a horse and wearing a military hat, shouting and raising his fist in the air. To the long list of Roosevelt's achievements we must add the invention of the presidential photo opportunity. He retired from politics in 1908 and went big-game hunting in Africa in 1909.

GEORGE W. BUSH'S WHITE HOUSE DRESS CODE

One of the first acts of George W. Bush on becoming president was to reinstate the White House dress code enforced by his father, President George Bush. All male White House staff are required to wear suits and ties, and women are required to wear "appropriate business attire." Under Bush's father, women were prohibited from wearing pants, but after lobbying by female staffers, George W. Bush's press secretary Ari Fleischer declared "the pantsuits can stay."

Bush's dress code is in marked contrast to the famously casually attired Clinton White House, where staffers often attended meetings in jeans and t-shirts. The implication is that Clinton and his staff did not show the proper respect for the office of president. As Joseph Curl of *The Washington Post* said: "Out are the 20-something, denim-wearing, pony-tailed Clintonites known for strewing pizza boxes throughout the halls, in are the 30- and 40-something, box-cut, scrubbed-clean, suit-and-tie-wearing Bushies."

Unlike Clinton, Bush runs the White House like a corporate CEO, and he is unfailingly punctual for meetings. Moreover, at the end of the working week, Bush is likely to head for his 1,600-acre ranch in Texas. There, he will be attired in jeans and Western shirt, a dress code which is more to Bush's own taste. Bush can look awkward in a suit, and has admitted that he does not like wearing them. During his 2000 election campaign, Bush posed for countless "meet the people" photo opportunities dressed in casual clothes. Yet, evidently, Bush considers that conveying the outward appearance of respectability is worth the discomfort of wearing a suit. And if he has to, then so do all his staff.

TONY BLAIR'S SHIRTS

Tony Blair, leader of Britain's Labour Party, was elected prime minister in 1997 and was reelected in 2001. Blair's usual attire is, of course, a suit, and he has made a point of supporting the British fashion industry by wearing clothes made by homegrown designers. This got him into trouble with the British press in 2002. Blair was photographed at a Europen summit meeting wearing a shirt by British designer Paul Smith. Nothing out of the ordinary there—except that the cuffs featured a drawing of a 1950s-style naked pinup girl.

The British press critized the prime minister, accusing him of trying to be daring or trendy when he was representing his country at an important

THE MAYOR AND LORD MAYOR OF LONDON

Each year, in the Lord Mayor's Show, the Lord Mayor of London parades through the streets in a gilded coach, dressed in fine robes and with the gold chain of office around his neck (center). Yet despite all the Lord Mayor's finery, modern-day London is actually governed by the mayor.

There has been a "Mayor of London" since the Middle Ages, but the position became a ceremonial one. The present-day Lord Mayor is the head of the Corporation of London, which controls "the City"—the "Square Mile" of the original city within its Roman walls. The Corporation of London owns public housing and parks, but it has no real governing powers.

In 2000, Ken Livingstone was elected London's first true mayor, with real powers over the whole city, which today extends for miles beyond its ancient boundaries. Livingstone wears a standard-issue politician's suit or, often, an open-necked shirt. This casual look suits his image as a man of the people.

meeting. A small mistake, perhaps, but it was poorly timed. Blair's policies were being heavily criticized in the media at the time, and the incident did some damage to his standing. Leaders may like to portray themselves as young, energetic, or original, but, especially in times of crisis, it is sometimes best to reflect—or appear to reflect—the dignity of their office.

NELSON MANDELA

During the **apartheid** regime in South Africa, Nelson Mandela led opposition to the government as leader of the African National Congress. He was imprisoned and spent 28 years in jail. In 1990, Mandela was released, and four years later, he was elected president in the country's first free and fair elections.

As South Africa's first black leader, Mandela vowed to make a change in South African society, and this applied equally to presidential dress. Mandela's brightly patterned and boldly colored shirts made him a symbol of the new South Africa, visibly different from the white men in suits who had gone before. The style of shirt was named the Madiba shirt, after Mandela's clan name.

In an interview with PBS television news, Mandela's personal assistant, Jessie Duarte, said:

"Well, throughout the time that I worked with him, there was always a battle about how the president should dress and look. I recall that we invited one of these upmarket image dresser people to come and talk to us…and they went through the whole thing about red tie, navy

Nelson Mandela is shown in one of his traditionally South African brightly patterned and boldly colored shirts.

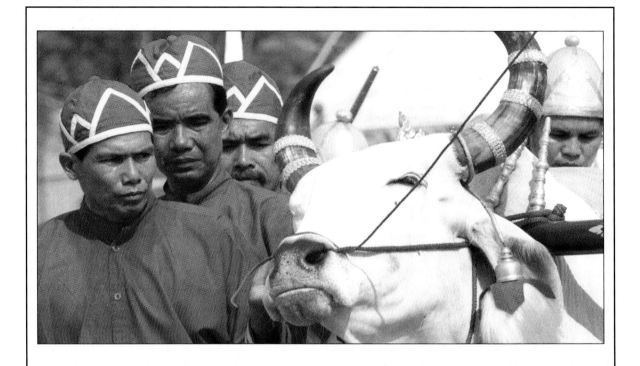

THE ANNUAL PLOWING CEREMONY: THAILAND

The Annual Plowing Ceremony takes place in May near the Grand Palace in Bangkok. The ceremony is of Brahman origin and has been performed since ancient times at the beginning of the new planting season. Today, the ceremony is held on the Annual Agriculturists Day to remind farmers of their importance in relation to the health of the nation and its economy.

During the ceremony, the amount of rainfall in the coming season is predicted. The Plowing Lord is offered a choice of three lengths of cloth, all looking identical: if he chooses the longest one there will be less rain; if his choice is the shortest one, rain will be plentiful; while the one of medium length indicates average rain. After donning the cloth, called *panung*, the Plowing Lord plows furrows in with a sacred plow of red and gold drawn by sacred white bulls and followed by four consecrated ladies who carry gold and silver baskets filled with rice seed. Brahmans walk alongside the plow.

blue…blue calms people down and all this stuff. And Madiba had a view. He said, 'This is Africa. Part of this three-piece suit belonged to the colonial era, when people were judged by what they wore, rather than who they were. If you were a man who wore a three-piece suit, then you would be respected.'

"His people—his own people—didn't have three-piece suits to wear; therefore, he needed to…dress the way the people dressed. He was very clear: 'I want to be comfortable. I want to dress like a man who is living in Africa, because that's where I live. I don't live in London, so I don't need a three-piece suit. When I visit London, I'll wear one if necessary.' Of course, he did visit London, and didn't wear a three-piece suit. He wore a Madiba shirt…It says a lot about Madiba…He is not a pretender. He wanted to be presented as who he was, and who he is."

FIDEL CASTRO

President Fidel Castro of Cuba came to power in a **Communist** revolution in 1959 and has ruled the country ever since. In 1962, the United States imposed a trade **embargo** on Cuba, which remains in effect to this day. Unable to trade with the U.S., Cuba found a willing partner in its Communist ally, the Soviet Union.

Castro's appearance, as much as his impassioned speeches, summed up his defiance toward the United States. He dressed, and continues to dress, not as a politician, but as a soldier, bearded and wearing the olive-drab uniform of a guerilla. Then, as now, Castro remains head of the Cuban one-party state and serves as a visible symbol of Communism.

With the collapse of the Soviet Union, Cuba lost a vital source of trade and financial assistance. Cuba's economy has suffered, and it has found itself isolated both from the United States and from the Communist world. In late 1995, Castro attempted to gain favor with both sides, making sure to convey the right image by wearing the appropriate clothing in each case.

In November of that year, Castro attended the 50th-anniversary celebration of the United Nations in New York. He took the opportunity to campaign for the ending of the U.S. trade embargo, arguing that lifting it would help the Cuban people and start to normalize relations between the two countries. As if to emphasize his new moderate stance, Castro was dressed, not in military fatigues, but in a conservative, dark business suit.

One month later, Castro visited China to discuss trade and ask for aid. Reverting to his trademark olive-drab uniform, Castro embraced Chinese president Jiang Zemin as if they were old comrades. It was, in fact, Castro's first visit to China. Cuba's close alliance with the Soviet Union had prevented his country from becoming too friendly with China in the past.

MAO TSE-TUNG

Mao Tse-tung (1893–1976) led the Communist revolution of 1949 and became the first head of state of the People's Republic of China. Mao brought in reforms in Chinese culture and society, including the elimination of clothing that denoted rank, and the introduction of the blue, high-collared, shirt-like jacket that became known as the Mao jacket.

Everyone from the Chairman to peasants wore the Mao jacket, visibly different from both traditional

Cuban president Fidel Castro, shown in March 2002, is wearing his trademark olive-drab military fatigues.

Chinese and Western dress. As such, it was a powerful symbol of unity and equality, even if that equality was often more imagined than real when opposition was brutally suppressed.

Mao resigned as head of state in 1959, but he remained Chairman of the Communist party and continued to wield power until his death. In 1966, Mao instigated the notorious Cultural Revolution, a movement to regain the revolutionary ideals that Mao felt were threatened by moderate reformers, such as Deng Xiaoping.

Mao appealed directly to the people with a huge billboard and poster campaign. Posters showed the Chairman in heroic pose and Mao jacket, above stirring slogans, such as "Urgently Forge Ahead and Bravely Advance with Great Leader Chairman Mao." The result was chaos, violence, and mass denunciations of real or imaginary "enemies of the people." Far from being a symbol of equality, the Mao jacket had become a symbol of state oppression.

After Mao's death, Deng and the reformers began to move away from Maoist beliefs, and the Mao billboards were gradually removed from China's public spaces. Today, China has embraced the free market, and billboards advertising cars, clothes, and computers are common. The youth of Beijing wear jeans or suits. Mao jackets are a thing of the past, worn only by the Party leaders who remain in power.

EUROPEAN JUDICIAL DRESS

Most judges throughout the world wear robes, a practice that derives from Europe in the Middle Ages. In the 13th and 14th centuries, the rulers of England, France, Spain, Portugal, and Austria appointed judges for the first time. Until then, the Church had run the courts.

As representatives of the monarch, judges dressed in the fur- and silk-lined robes of a nobleman. Robes changed according to the seasons, usually green in the summer and violet in the winter, with red reserved for special occasions.

In 1685, judges and **barristers** began to wear black robes as a sign of mourning for the death of Charles II. They have apparently never gotten over it, as barristers' gowns remain black to this day. Largely because many of the world's legal systems—including America's—are based on English law, black is the usual color of judges' robes in countries where they are worn.

Wigs and Gowns

In the higher courts, English judges and barristers wear not only gowns, but also wigs, a practice that dates from the 1680s. Powdered white or grey wigs were the fashion of the day, but the legal profession has never stopped wearing them. Barristers wear short, simple wigs, but senior judges wear long, elaborate horsehair wigs weighing several pounds. In some higher courts and on ceremonial occasions, barristers and judges also wear the clothing of a

THE BLACK CAP

One piece of English judicial wear was eliminated in the 20th century—the judge's black cap, or "judgment cap," which was worn when pronouncing a sentence of death. The cap represented that worn for mourning by the Israelites, Greeks, Romans, and Anglo-Saxons.

The cap is not worn today because England abolished the death penalty in 1965. A high-profile murder trial of 1953 helped to turn public opinion against the death penalty. Derek Bentley, an 18 year old, was sentenced to death for his part in the shooting of a policeman. Bentley's friend had pulled the trigger, but since the murderer was 16 and too young to hang, Bentley was executed in his place. Bentley's family conducted a long campaign to clear his name, and his appeal was finally heard in 1998. Bentley's conviction was overturned 45 years too late to save him.

fashionable 18th-century gentleman—a formal jacket known as a bar jacket, a wing collar, and neck bands.

The strict guidelines for judges' apparel was set out in a 1992 document issued by the Lord Chancellor and the Lord Chief Justice:

"When sitting in the Court of Appeal (Criminal Division), High Court judges, like other members of the Court of Appeal, wear a black silk gown and a short wig, as they do in Divisional Court. When dealing with criminal business at first instance in the winter, a High Court judge wears the scarlet robe of the ceremonial dress but without the scarlet cloth and fur mantle. When dealing with criminal business in the summer, the judge wears a similar scarlet robe, but with silk rather than fur facings. A Queen's Bench judge trying civil cases in winter wears a black robe faced with fur, a black scarf and **girdle** and a scarlet **tippet**; in summer, a violet robe faced with silk, with the black scarf and girdle and scarlet tippet. On red letter days (which include the sovereign's birthday and certain saints' days), all judges wear the scarlet robe for the appropriate season."

In the same year, the legal profession debated whether to abolish the wearing of wigs. After months of consideration, it was decided that wigs would be kept. As Lord Donaldson, a senior judge, put it, there was no urgent need to start "discarding something [that] has been out of date for at least a century."

The countries of the Commonwealth, which based their attire, as well as their legal system, on English law, have followed the practice of wearing wigs to some degree. In Australia, judges and barristers wear legal dress with wigs for most appearances at federal courts and at higher state courts, but not for lower state and local courts.

JUDICIAL DRESS IN THE UNITED STATES

The attire of judges in the United States was a subject debated by the founding

REBELLION IN THE RANKS

The U.S. Supreme Court's Chief Justice William H. Rehnquist broke with the tradition of black gowns in 1995 by adding four gold flashes to each sleeve of his gown. The military-style flashes came to the media's attention during the Senate impeachment trial of Bill Clinton, when it was assumed they were a sign of Rehnquist's support of the military in opposing President Clinton. But the truth was far stranger. In 1994, Rehnquist had seen a production of Gilbert and Sullivan's comic opera *Iolanthe*. He took a liking to the gown worn by the Lord Chancellor character and had it copied.

Rehnquist claimed the gown was a joke, but his critics saw it as a sign of his desire to dominate the Supreme Court, in opposition to the long-standing notion of equality among the justices. Although Rehnquist is known as a conservative, he is also something of a renegade and an individualist, who has handed down some surprisingly liberal rulings. He does not always respect rules of attire either—in the 1970s, he was known for wearing desert boots under his judge's robes.

fathers. Thomas Jefferson argued against the wearing of both robes and wigs, stating that he was against "any needless official apparel" and that English judges in their wigs reminded him of "mice peeping out of **oakum**." Alexander Hamilton favored both robe and wig, while Aaron Burr favored the robe, but was against the wig. Burr's preference was the one they decided to adopt for the U.S. federal courts.

CLEAVAGE IN CANADA

The dress of lawyers in court was thrust into the headlines in a case in Canada in 1995. During the hearing of a minor assault case in Windsor, Ontario, Justice Micheline Rawlins took exception to the attire of defense lawyer Laura Joy and ordered her out of the court to change into something more modest. "I cannot hear your argument until you change your clothes," Rawlins instructed the lawyer.

On that morning, Joy was wearing a pinstriped jacket and trousers with a white polyester V-neck top. It was reported that her attire would be considered perfectly appropriate for office wear, but, unfortunately for Joy, Justice Rawlins held strong views on the subject of correct attire. Explaining her actions, Rawlins said: "Whatever lawyers wear should not distract the court from their legal presentations. I don't want to see bra straps. I don't want to see cleavage. I don't want to see belly buttons. Is that too much to ask in a court of law?"

Canada follows English practice in requiring lawyers to wear black gowns for appearances in higher courts, such as the national, superior, and federal appeals courts, but not for the provincial courts that handle most minor criminal cases.

Today, state judges also wear black robes, but many states did not adopt the custom until well into the 20th century. Until the 1950s, Florida's justices sat behind the bench unrobed, wearing plain business suits. At least one justice was against robes. Richard W. Ervin was appointed as the 55th justice in 1964, and, despite his opposition, was required to wear a black robe. Ervin, who became known as "The Robe-Shy Judge," said: "It always seemed incongruous to me, a Florida cracker, born in Carrabelle, that I should be enrobed. I was awfully glad we weren't bewigged!"

MILITARY DRESS UNIFORM

At the time of the American Revolution, soldiers were not always issued with a full uniform, and since all the uniforms were tailor-made, there were variations from one uniform to the next. As a result, it was important to clearly distinguish one army from another with brightly colored sashes and jackets. The disadvantage was that soldiers in bright uniforms, like the British "redcoats" in the American Revolution, were easy targets for their enemies.

At the start of World War I, brightly colored uniforms were still worn in combat. French infantry soldiers in 1914 were dressed in blue coats with gold buttons, red **epaulets**, and red trousers. Even the "field gray" uniforms of the German army sported colorful piping. German cavalrymen also wore plumed helmets in battle.

By 1916, these colorful uniforms had disappeared. The French adopted plain-colored "horizon blue" uniforms. Brightly colored uniforms were too good a target for snipers and were impractical for muddy trench warfare. Durable and practical, drab-colored uniforms soon became an essential requirement

A United States Marines corporal, dressed for a 1985 parade in the dress blue B uniform. It has a dark-blue tunic, trimmed with red, and lighter blue trousers with a red stripe. He has two citation ribbons on his left breast, and rifle and pistol proficiency badges.

THE COLDSTREAM GUARDS

The Coldstream Guards, formed in 1650, is the oldest continually operating regiment in Britain. It has served in every conflict since England's Civil War, from the Napoleonic Wars to both world wars and the Gulf War. Although the men of the regiment have been honored for their valor countless times, it is for their ceremonial duties that they are known to the public. They form part of the Queen's Guard and can be seen at such occasions as Trooping the Color, state visits, and the daily Changing of the Guard at Buckingham Palace. A company of Guards is stationed permanently in London for these ceremonial duties.

The Coldstream Guards' famous dress uniform consists of a bright red tunic, tall bearskin hat (with a red plume to distinguish them from other Guards regiments), and navy blue trousers with a red stripe. The bearskin was adopted in 1831. The present-day dress uniform is basically 19th-century, with a few 20th-century modifications, such as the elimination of capes in 1948, when ceremonial dress was reintroduced after World War II.

for modern warfare. Dress uniforms from this point onward were in contrast to combat or service uniforms and remained in their 19th-century form.

The modern soldier probably has four or five uniforms, including a general-service uniform, uniforms for specialized tasks, and a combat uniform. The dress uniform is used for special occasions, such as public parades or visits by dignitaries, and in most cases, is directly descended from the colorful general service uniform of the 19th century, such as the dress blues of the U.S. Marines, or the red coats and bearskins of the British Coldstream Guards. Dress uniform can also be worn in place of civilian formalwear at dinners and events.

THE UNITED STATES MARINES

Like other branches of the military, the U.S. Marines has a range of uniforms for different occasions. There are three categories of uniform worn by all U.S. Marines: blue dress (or blue-white dress for officers), service, and utility. Dress uniforms are further divided into four types.

Blue dress "A" is the most formal uniform and is used for formal or semiformal social functions and for important military occasions. These include parades, ceremonies, reviews, and visits by U.S. or foreign civil or military officials. Blue dress "A" consists of a blue dress coat and trousers (skirt for women) in wool or **gabardine**. Large medals are worn with this uniform.

In summer, officers wear the blue-white dress uniform: the same blue dress jacket, but white trousers (or skirt). If the ceremony also includes enlisted Marines, officers do not wear the blue-white uniform, but instead wear the same blue dress uniform as enlisted personnel.

Medals are worn only at the most important occasions. For other parades and ceremonies, or for informal social functions, marines wear ribbons instead of medals, and this is known as blue dress "B." Unlike the "A" uniform, the blue or blue-white "B" dress uniform can be used as the **uniform of the day** and can also be worn by Marines on leave.

CHAPTER 3

Civilians

The last century has seen changes in what was considered proper for life's more formal occasions, but the basic principle of wearing distinctive clothing for special events has remained remarkably consistent through the decades.

MEN'S DAY- AND EVENINGWEAR

From the late 19th century to the 1920s, men's formalwear was established. There were two unvarying uniforms for day- and eveningwear. Eveningwear consisted of a black tailcoat, white bow tie, black or white vest, and black trousers, with a white, heavily starched shirt. As *The Ball Room Guide*, a Victorian **etiquette** manual, put it in 1860:

"When a gentleman is invited out for the evening, he is under no embarrassment as to what he shall wear. He has not to sit

Fred Astaire (right) is in top hat and tails (1935). Hollywood's depiction of "high society" and the actors' dress at award ceremonies, such as the Oscars, popularized formalwear.

45

down and consider whether he shall wear blue or pink, or whether the Joneses will notice if he wears the same attire three times running. Fashion has ordained for him that he shall always be attired in a black dress suit in the evening, only allowing him a white waistcoat [vest] as an occasional relief to his toilette. His necktie must be white or light colored. An excess of jewelry is to be avoided, but he may wear gold or diamond studs, and a watch chain. He may also wear a flower in his buttonhole, for this is one of the few allowable devices by which he

THE DINNER JACKET

The dinner jacket was believed to have been first worn at formal occasions by the Prince of Wales, later to be Edward VII, in the 1880s. Until then, gentlemen had worn tails for formal events, but the Prince popularized the tailless, satin-lapelled black dinner jacket.

The dinner jacket made its first appearance in the U.S. in 1886, at the Autumn Ball of the Tuxedo Club in Tuxedo Park, New York.

Tuxedo Park, 40 miles (65 km) west of New York City, was a playground for the rich and famous of the day. In 1885, James Brown Potter of the Tuxedo Club had visited London and met the Prince of Wales, who had worn a dinner jacket to a party. On returning to the U.S., Potter related this to one of the club's members, Griswold Lorillard, who startled the assembled company at the 1886 ball by attending in the new tailless dinner jacket.

By the turn of the 20th century, the tuxedo had become established at society functions. It was then introduced to the public and popularized by the early stars of Hollywood, both in movies and at public appearances, such as the Oscars. As the century progressed, the tuxedo came to be adopted as the standard male formal wear by all classes of society, worn at special events, such as company dinners, charity functions, and high school proms.

An aristocratic family in 1962 poses for a family portrait in fashionable and elegant eveningwear. The husband is wearing a red dinner jacket with medals. The young boy is wearing a kilt, which implies that the family is of Scottish descent.

THE COCKTAIL DRESS

In the 1920s, a new development in women's formal attire was the appearance of the cocktail dress. Cocktail parties were given in the late afternoon, going on until the early evening, and a new dress was invented that sat between formal eveningwear and more casual daytime wear. A cocktail dress is usually shorter than an evening dress, but it can be just as showy. Cocktail dresses in the 1920s were often in shimmering fabrics or embroidered with sequins or jewels.

may brighten his attire…Plain and simple as the dress is, it is a sure test of a gentlemanly appearance. The man who dines in evening dress every night of his life looks easy and natural in it, whereas the man who takes to it late in life generally succeeds in looking like a waiter."

Daywear consisted of a morning suit, which first appeared in the early 1880s. The morning suit was a compromise between the rigidly formal frock suit and the looser, more casual sack suit, which was not considered formal enough for daytime social and business occasions. The morning suit retained the gray striped trousers, black coat, and vest of the frock suit, but the lapels were narrower and the hemline of the coat made rounder. A top hat was no longer considered essential, as it had been with the frock suit, and **Windsor ties** were increasingly worn in place of bow ties. Traditional day and eveningwear is retained today only for the most formal white-tie events. Today, for the vast majority of formal events, men wear a dinner jacket (also known as a tuxedo).

WOMEN'S FORMALWEAR

Now, as in 1900, women wear long evening dresses for the most formal and important occasions. Unlike male formal attire, the exact design of women's eveningwear has evolved according to changing tastes and fashions.

In the early 1900s, the belle-epoque style meant sumptuous fabrics, heavy embroidery, and a train. This was the acceptable dress for women attending events at the British royal court, and it was adopted for formal events in Europe and North America. In the first and second decades of the century, Oriental or Gypsy fashions were a big influence, and flowing fabrics and wide sleeves were incorporated into ladies' formal wear.

WEDDINGS

For some people, the only time they will wear formal dress is at a wedding. Many people like to mark the special occasion with formal clothing. There are conventions about what the wedding party and guests should wear, according to the formality, time of day, and time of year of the wedding. But there are no longer any hard-and-fast rules, and what the wedding party and guests wear is up to the taste of the bride and groom. The degree of formality is set by the bride's dress. If she wears a dress with a train, the wedding is considered formal.

COMING-OF-AGE CEREMONIES

In many cultures around the world, children have to pass through a ceremony before they are considered adults. Some of these ceremonies are religious, such as the *bar mitzvah*, or *bat mitzvah*, that Jewish boys and girls attend at 13 years of age. In the Catholic faith, children make their First Communion, usually after the age of seven or eight. Upper-class girls in North America attend debutante balls in their mid-teens, and around the world, particularly in North America, high school seniors attend proms and

The photographer straightens the bride's long train at this formal daytime wedding. The groom and his attendants are all wearing dinner jackets with satin lapels, black bow ties, and corsages that match the bridal bouquet.

graduation ceremonies. For most of these events, participants wear formal or ceremonial dress.

First Communion

Girls making their First Communion traditionally wear an elaborate white dress similar to a wedding dress. This practice is followed to this day, but it is not required, and girls will often instead wear a stylish formal outfit. The

DRESS CODES

A guide to the most common dress codes that you will find on invitations, in descending order of formality:

White Tie or Ultraformal Men wear full evening dress for evening events or morning suits for daytime events. Women wear long gowns.

Black Tie or Formal Men wear dinner jackets, women wear cocktail or long dresses, or dressy separates. For some more fashionable events, men might dispense with a tie and instead wear a black shirt with a dinner jacket.

Black Tie Optional or Black Tie Invited Men can wear a dinner jacket or a dark suit and tie. Women wear cocktail or long dresses, or dressy separates.

Creative Black Tie Allows for trendy or unusual interpretations of formal wear.

Semiformal Usually dinner jackets are not required, nor are long dresses. However, an evening event (after 6 PM) still dictates dark suits for men and cocktail dresses for women. Daytime semiformal events mean a suit for men and a short dress or dressy suit for women.

Cocktail Attire Short, elegant dresses for women and dark suits for men.

Dressy Casual Usually no jeans or shorts.

Informal Can mean the same as casual. But some form of decorum and good taste should prevail for a wedding or other special event. Women should probably wear a dress and men a stylish-looking shirt and trousers.

Casual Generally anything goes.

white of Communion attire symbolizes the child's purity. At the turn of the 20th century, boys also wore formal white Communion suits, but this practice is now rare. By the 1920s and 1930s, boys more commonly wore black or dark suits. These were often specially made and rather old-fashioned, with short trousers or **knickerbockers**. As tastes changed, so did

Communion attire, and boys wore a suit and tie in the style of the day, as they do for the most part today.

Debutante Balls

Debutante balls are events marking the entrance of upper-class girls into adult society. They are originally derived from the presentation of girls at the royal courts, and they continue to this day in North America and Europe. Girls traditionally wear long white dresses and carry flowers, symbolizing both their purity and their availability for marriage. Debutante dresses must have sleeves and be without **décolletage**.

Some debutante balls are given for the debuts of individual girls, and parents can spend tens of thousands of dollars on their daughters' parties. Other girls attend large, highly formal, and elaborate balls, where a large number of girls debut together.

At the most prestigious and formal balls in the United States and Europe, rules dictate that each girl must be accompanied by two male escorts, one civilian, in black tie, and the other military, usually with a military school cadet, in full military dress uniform.

High School Graduation

Graduation ceremonies are a 20th-century invention. In many U.S. states, high schools were not established until the late 19th century, and attendance at school was not enforced until the early years of the 20th century. Most schools have graduation ceremonies that require graduates to wear academic dress similar to those of graduating university students.

Prom Night

In their senior year, usually in spring, students also attend high school proms. These dance parties are a kind of equivalent of debutante balls, except on a

This teenage debutante is wearing a simple but elegant white dress, along with short white gloves. She is wearing simple jewelry to complement the dress, avoiding any loud, garish decoration.

This young couple is dancing at their prom. The boy is wearing a traditional black suit and tie, while the girl is wearing a formal dress. The corsage around her wrist was a gift from her date. He is wearing a matching boutonniere.

lower social level, marking the end of school and the start of adulthood. Unlike debutante balls, however, proms are equally important for boys and girls. Boys usually wear black tie. Girls generally wear long gowns, often light-colored, but unlikely to be white, and wear a corsage of flowers. In most cases, long gowns are not required and girls wear whatever formal or elaborate dress they can afford, perhaps embroidered, sequined, or of fine material and in keeping with the fashion of the day.

NATIONAL DRESS

Countries throughout the world have national dress that is worn on national days and at other important events. Often, it is a version of traditional dress that may be centuries old. The national dress in most cases is worn only for

BRIDAL BOUQUETS AND CORSAGES

The custom of a bride carrying a bouquet as she walks down the aisle may date back to the ancient Romans. Some historians say Roman brides carried bunches of fragrant herbs and flowers on their wedding day to ward off evil spirits. And the ancient Greeks, they say, carried ivy as a symbol of fidelity.

Corsages are also often worn at weddings, particularly by various members of the bridal party, but are more strongly associated with proms. The giving of corsages (and flowers in general) has a ritual dimension: it shows that the giver considers that person special and that he or she is asking them to enter into a special relationship, even if it is for only one evening. Acceptance of the corsage indicates the acceptance of this invitation.

The boutonniere is like a small version of the corsage, usually given by the woman to her partner for the evening after he has presented her with a corsage. It is pinned on his lapel.

ceremonial occasions, although in some countries, national dress is worn in place of formalwear or may even be worn every day.

In Austria and southern Germany, women wear a *dirndl*, a 19th-century outfit of a lacy white blouse with puffed sleeves and a full, round skirt, traditionally decorated with a pattern of flowers and red stripes. In the 20th century, the *dirndl* ceased to be normal everyday wear and is now usually reserved for special occasions. Some women wear the *dirndl* on a more regular basis, for any event that requires a degree of dressing up, such as a party or an outing to the opera or theater.

In Scotland, the poet Robert Burns (1759–1796) is celebrated at Burns suppers held on or around his birthday, January 25. Burns suppers range from informal events in people's homes to highly elaborate formal dinners, with a strict order of

These Californian Scotsmen are wearing traditional kilts during their participation in the Scottish Highland Games at Santa Rosa. The kilts are combined with modern attire—the t-shirts and sneakers are not traditional.

ceremony that includes readings from Burns, songs, speeches, drinking Scotch whisky, and eating a traditional Scottish meal. **Haggis** is always served, and is "piped in" to the dining room, carried by the chef behind a bagpiper wearing full Highland dress. The master of ceremonies then reads Burns' poem "To a Haggis," making the first cut as he reaches the line "an' cut you up wi' ready slight."

Full Highland dress is the Scottish equivalent of black tie, and can be worn by Scots in place of black tie at all formal events. The top half of the outfit is a modified version of black tie, worn with a "Prince Charlie" jacket, a black jacket with cutaways and decorated with silver buttons. In place of trousers there is a kilt, worn with a **sporran**, knee socks with tasseled **flashes**, and laced **brogue** shoes. A ceremonial sheathed dagger, or *skean-dhu*, is also worn on the leg inside the top of the sock. Kilts are strictly male attire, and women usually wear a blouse and tartan skirt for formal events.

ACADEMIC DRESS

Today's academic dress has its origins in the Middle Ages, when students in unheated rooms wore gowns and hoods for warmth. In the time of England's Henry VIII, regulations were brought in requiring students to wear gowns. The fashion of the time was for rich, colorful linings, and this is reflected in the linings and trims of modern doctorate gowns. The gowns were made of silk or **stuff**. Modern gowns are made of synthetics or wool, with silk or satin used on some facings and sleeve linings.

Universities in Britain, Ireland, the Commonwealth, and to some extent the United States follow the pattern of Oxford and Cambridge gowns. In the mid-1800s, the American Council on Education formulated an "Inter-Collegiate Code" for academic dress in the U.S., which was updated in 1932. This dress code is largely in effect to this day. The code sets out rules, such as the trim colors to be used on the hoods, each color representing a particular field of study. Law, for example, is purple and music is pink. In the later 20th century, some universities, including Cornell, Yale, Stanford, Harvard, and the University of California, broke away and implemented their own color schemes. As a general rule, the higher the degree, the longer and more sumptuous and colorful is the gown. Higher degrees are also indicated by longer hoods at American universities, doctors' hoods being the longest at 4 feet (1.2 m).

Bill and Hillary Clinton are at their daughter Chelsea's graduation ceremony at Stanford University in 2001. The color and design of Chelsea's gown indicate the degree she was awarded—a B.A. in History.

Gowns are normally worn only at graduations in the United States, but until well into the 20th century, students at Oxford and Cambridge in Britain had to wear gowns at all times, even in public outside the university. Today, the students do not have to wear gowns all the time, however, they are still required to wear them for special occasions, such as formal college dinners, graduations, and examinations.

At Oxford, faculty members have a plain gown known as "undress" and a "dress" gown reserved for ceremonial occasions. Doctors' gowns are scarlet, and lower degrees are black, with brightly colored facings and linings. At special occasions, such as Encaenia—the annual ceremony awarding honorary degrees—university officials parade through the streets to the ceremony in all their finery. The chancellor of the university has a particularly long gown, which is held by a page boy as he walks at the head of the procession.

FUNERAL DRESS

As with weddings, there are some basic conventions for funeral attire, but these will, of course, vary across different cultures. Certainly in most Christian societies, black is the color of mourning, and for a funeral, reasonably stylish attire should be worn. The dress of a contemporary funeral gathering, although likely to be subdued and neat, stands in strong contrast to the elaborate costumes of mourners in the first half of the 20th century. The most extreme example of those practices can be seen in newspaper photographs of the funeral of the British King George VI, when the women of the royal family concealed their faces under long, heavy mourning veils and dressed completely in black from head to toe.

DRESSING FOR A JOURNEY TO ETERNITY

The Japanese traditionally dress their dead in "grave clothes," a hood and a money pouch containing six pieces of money. That this costume has a close resemblance to the traveling outfit of ancient times is not a coincidence: the *shinishozoku* can be regarded as the costume for starting on a journey to eternity. The six pieces of money in the pouch are said to be used as a ferriage for crossing the Japanese Styx.

GLOSSARY

Apartheid a system of strict racial segregation in South Africa

Appliqué a decorative shape cut out from one material and stitched on top of another

Barrister a lawyer who presents cases in court

Belle Epoque meaning "beautiful age"; a period of high artistic or cultural development

Bodice the upper part of a woman's dress

Brogue a heavy, coarse shoe

Cambric a type of fine, white linen, originally made in Cambrai in northern France

Chapel train the most popular train length for a wedding gown, extending 3 to 4 feet (90–120 cm) behind the gown

Chiffon a sheer fabric, usually silk

Commonwealth an association of self-governing states united in a common allegiance

Communism a totalitarian system of government in which a single authoritarian party controls state-owned means of production

Coup a sudden and often successful takeover

Cummerbund broad waist sash worn under a dinner jacket in place of a vest

Décolletage a low-cut neckline

Depose to remove from high position

Edwardian characteristic of the reign of the British king, Edward VII (1901–1910)

Embargo an order prohibiting commerce between one country and another

Epaulet an ornamental fringed shoulder pad

Ermine any of several weasels whose fur is white in winter

Etiquette manners or proper behavior prescribed by authority to be observed in social or official life

Fedora a low, soft, felt hat with the crown creased lengthwise

Flash British military term meaning a colored piece of cloth (or tassle) that is a distinguishing emblem

Gabardine a sturdy, tightly woven fabric of wool, cotton, or rayon twill

Girdle a waist belt worn with some robes

Habit a costume worn for horseback riding

Haggis a Scottish dish in which the minced heart, liver, and lungs of a sheep or calf are combined with oatmeal and seasonings and then boiled in the animal's stomach

Hussars soldiers of a light cavalry regiment belonging to any of various European countries

Knickerbockers loose-fitting, short trousers gathered at or near the knee

Lance a steel-tipped spear

Morning suit men's daytime dress for formal

occasions; usually consists of a winged-collar shirt, vest, and formal trousers

MP Member of Parliament (British)

Nosegay a small bunch of flowers

Oakum loosely twisted hemp or jute fiber used in caulking to prevent leaks

Regency the governing of a country on behalf of a king who has not yet reached the age of majority

Reserve minimum price for an object at auction

Scepter a staff or baton carried by a sovereign as an emblem of authority

Sporran a pouch worn in front of a man's kilt in full Highland dress

Stuff a finished wool or worsted material

Sweep train the shortest train on a wedding dress, barely sweeping the floor

Tippet a short cape worn about the shoulders consisting of hanging bands of fabric

Tissue a delicate, sheer fabric

Tulle stiffened silk, nylon, or rayon

Twill a fabric whose weave gives the appearance of diagonal lines

Uniform of the day a particular working uniform to be worn by all staff, it may change according to the season or the day's tasks

Victorian of, or characteristic of, the reign of Queen Victoria

Windsor tie a broad necktie, usually tied in a loose bow

TIMELINE

1785 English lawyers wear black robes in mourning for the death of Charles II.

1831 Bearskin hat first worn by Coldstream Guards.

1880s Morning suit first worn.

1886 Griswold Lorillard introduces the dinner jacket to the United States.

1900–1910 Belle Epoque style dominates European and American fashions.

1901 McKinley assassinated; Theodore Roosevelt becomes U.S. President.

1902 Coronation of Edward VII and Queen Alexandra of Britain.

1916 Drab field uniforms adopted by World War I soldiers.

1920s Cocktail dress introduced; tuxedo worn throughout Europe and North America.

1926 Emperor Hirohito succeeds to the Japanese throne.

1930 Coronation of Haile Selassie.

1932 Revised version of U.S. "Inter-Collegiate Code" of academic dress published.

1936 Publication of "Dress and Insignia Worn at His Majesty's Court."

1946 Hirohito denies his divinity, and dons a suit and hat.

1948 Cape dropped from Coldstream Guards' dress uniform, the last design change in the 20th century.

1950s Paris fashion houses dominate formalwear. Suits and separates first worn as female formal attire.

1953 Coronation of Elizabeth II of Britain.

1954 Coronation of King Hussein of Jordan.

1959 Fidel Castro leads Communist revolution in Cuba.

1960 John F. Kennedy elected U.S. president.

1962 United States imposes trade embargo on Cuba.

1965 Death penalty abolished in England.

1966 Mao Tse-Tung instigates the Cultural Revolution.

1976 Jimmy Carter elected U.S. president.

1977 Coronation of self-styled Emperor Bokassa.

1981 Wedding of Prince Charles and Lady Diana Spencer.

1986 Queen Elizabeth II stops wearing military dress uniform at Trooping the Color.

1992 English legal profession rejects the scrapping of wigs and gowns.

1994 Nelson Mandela elected president of South Africa.

1995 Fidel Castro wears a business suit for a visit to New York; Chief Justice Rehnquist adds stripes to his black judicial gown.

1997 Charity auction of Princess Diana's formal gowns; death of Princess Diana; Tony Blair elected British Prime Minister.

2000 George W. Bush elected U.S. president.

FURTHER INFORMATION

BOOKS

Buxbaum, Gerda, ed. *Icons of Fashion: The Twentieth Century.* Munich: Prestel, 1999.

Ewing, Elizabeth. *History of 20th Century Fashion (revised edition).* New York: Quite Specific Media Group Ltd., 2002.

Harrold, Robert. *Folk Costumes of the World.* London: Cassell, 1999.

Knightly, Charles. *The Customs and Ceremonies of Britain.* London: Thames and Hudson, 1986.

Lurie, Alison. *The Language of Clothes.*
London: Bloomsbury, 1992.

Mansfield, Alan. *Ceremonial Costume: Court, Civil and Civic Costume from 1660 to the Present Day.* London: Black, 1980.

Seeling, Charlotte. *Fashion: The Century of Design 1900–1999.* Cologne: Könemann, 1999.

ONLINE SOURCES

British and Commonwealth Academic Dress
www.clark.edu
A guide to the color codes of academic gowns.

The Presidents of the United States
www.whitehouse.gov/history/presidents
Various history links and biographies of every United States president.

The World of Royalty
www.royalty.nu
History and current news of royalty around the world.

Official Web Site of the U.S. Marines.
www.usmc.mil
The History and Museums Division has interesting articles about traditional ceremonies and attire.

The Wedding Channel
www.weddingchannel.com
Browse through different styles of wedding gowns, bridesmaid dresses, and accessories.

ABOUT THE AUTHOR

Lewis Lyons was educated at Oxford and London and started his career at a London community newspaper. He spent seven years in the United States, for the most part in New York City, where he headed a photo agency, edited a computer magazine, and wrote on technology, music, business, and society. His recent publications include books and articles about the Internet, the soccer World Cup, and the U.S. Coast Guard.

INDEX